HOME GROAN

HOME GROAN

Cynical Puns
and
Other Wordplay

By M. Rose Pierce

Carroll & Graf Publishers, Inc.
New York

First Carroll & Graf edition 1993

Carroll & Graf Publishers, Inc.
260 Fifth Avenue
New York, NY 10001

Library of Congress Cataloging-in-Publication Data

Pierce, M. Rose.
    Home groan: cynical puns and other wordplay / M. Rose Pierce — 1st
ed.
       p. cm.
    ISBN 0-7867-0012-2 : $8.95
    1. Puns and punning. 2. Play on words. I. Title.
PN6231.P8P54 1993
818'.5402—dc20   93-14497
                                                     CIP

Book design by Studio 31

Manufactured in the United States of America

FOREWORD

Let's get write to wit.

Part of the fun in the unending game of wordplay is coping with one of spoken language's limitations: that it's hard to say several things at once and make sense. Poems are admired for evading that limitation; puns are abhorred for battering it down. Even dictionaries define a punner as a "rammer." The involuntary groans puns elicit — the shock of recognition in the pit of the stomach — testify to puns' power, exactly as do involuntary laughs to jokes. Much the same can be said for puns' specialized kin, including Tom Swifties, Passed Participles, and even Hinky Pinkies. Any punchline can succeed or fail depending on its context; all evoke a response.

Long contexts rarely work. One of the few exceptions is Roger Zelazny's novel, *The Lord of Light*. The first hundred pages or so lead inexorably to the climactic line, "Then the fit hit the Shan." Even the shortest stories ("set-ups"), concocted to lead irrelevantly to the preset punchline, no matter how ingenious, are scorned by purist punsters. Overfamiliar examples include the ones whose punchlines are

"Boy-foot bear with teak of Chan!" and "It's a long way to tip a Raree!", not to mention the family farm named *Focus* because "that's where the sons raise meat." For the most elaborate lines, no rational context seems possible. Is a crazy context better than none? Long contexts will probably survive, outlasting their welcome, despite the efforts of Reginald Bretnor, Poul Anderson, the late Randall Garrett, etc., in decades of random serial installments of the adventures through space and time of one Ferdinand Feghoot (*Magazine of Fantasy and Science Fiction*).

In general, the shorter the context, the more *pungent* the result. The endpoint: a single word or phrase creates the context, the *punch*line defends it. Two principal types are: 1) Wileys or daffynitions (surrealistic, made famous by Johnny Hart, many years before he put Wiley in *B.C.*), and 2) Bierces or scoffinitions (realistic and/or cynical, made notorious by Ambrose Bierce in *Devil's Dictionary*). Among the more famous daffynitions (not from Wiley's Hart nor vice versa): incongruous — "where laws are made"; shampoo — "Winnie the Impostor"; ramshackle — "sheep fetter." Most herein are of the Biercely persuasion, as one would expect from their origin in the soon to be published *Cynic's Dictionary* ("More on this later," said Tom haltingly).

Appropriately for a dictionary, our words define themselves; appropriately for good bathroom reading, our themes expose themselves. Here are a few daffynitions and a scoffinition to prepare us for our groans, excerpted from *The Cynic's Dictionary*.

pun *v.* 1) Rejoyce. 2) Leave no term ungroaned. 3) Play games with cognitive dissonance, As the Word Turns. 4) Ask one word to do the work of two; receive two meanings for the price of one. Less linguistic mining than serendipity. 5) At best, find the piece which simultaneously fills two gaps, fits two puzzles. 6) At worst, take care of the sounds and let the sense take care of itself. Examples of such *sonic gematria* (justly disdained by purists) range from Ferdinand Feghoot's adventures to Jean Pierre Brisset's flights of folly. All such have contributed to the game's ill repute — especially among those unable to play. Or are they afraid to push the punnic button? Punning is neither illegal, immoral, nor fattening, and it's free.

"Those most dislike puns who are least able to utter them." — Edgar Allen Poe.

"I never knew an enemy to puns who was not an ill-natured man." — Charles Lamb.

pun *n.* 1) Is mightier than the word. 2) Jester's test of fool's tool. 3) Part of Shakespeare's stock in trade. ("Ask for me tomorrow and you shall find me a grave man." *Romeo & Juliet*) 4) Pope trope, from Simon Peter to Alexander. The former: "You're 'Rocky', and on this rock I will build my church." (*Matt.* 16:18.) The latter: "Where a Word, like the tongue of a jackdraw, speaks twice as much by being split." (*Peri Bathous*, ch.10). 5) At best, word jazz. Where a jingle of phonemes becomes a jangle of themes; a jungle of seemings, a juggle of meanings; chance transfigured by choice, where virtue is in it's own reword. 6) Epigram epitomized; comedy condensed; even an old maxim minimized. 7) Linguistic fusion energy. As close kin to portmanteau words and Passed Participles as to the epigram, paradox, and oxymoron. 8) Where the meanings of magic overlap: verbal legerdemain; playfully eliciting the visceral shock of recognition; manipulating minds. 9) Too often, a groan of contention.

Scotland Yard's drug intelligence agents wear a distinctive necktie depicting a hypodermic needle clutched by a broken-winged bird: yes, "ill eagle."

A groan signals a win in the punster's game, like a laugh in the jester's. The same pun can win or lose, depending on how precise its timing, how appropriate its dual context — and how many of its audience understand it.

A pun's beauty is in the Oy! of the beholder. Arguably, the phrase *"pun not intended"* is usually false (fun not intended?). Herein, puns' prey is the cliché. Game tools: 1) collections of clichés; 2) a rhyming dictionary; 3) a range of topics; ruthless pruning. The method guarantees rediscovery of old favorites. But among punsters, independent invention is the rule not the exception.

punster *n.* Cunning linguist, whose tongue plays games provoking moans and groans. Punsters do it just for the stun of it. As with the spider, the female of the species is deadlier than the male; alas, unlike the spider, rarer.

Our prey is the clichémonger: "In your heart you know he's trite." Our preferred demise? Digesting.

Hinky Pinky *n.phr.* Paradigm by a rhyme. Proposed definition by sound repetition. At best, ingenuity excuses the game; at worst, nothing can. Examples abound in this dictionary.

Tom Swifties *n.phr.* 1) Adverbs' holiday: "I've got my own burden to bear," said Jesus crossly. (Quoted by Peter S. Beagle, 7/87.) "Frederick's of Hollywood now boasts a bra museum," said Tom fittingly. "It's dark," said Tom delightedly. Moments later, "How's this feel?" Tom asked indifferently. 2) Verbs' festival: "Sex is great!," Tom ejaculated. (Source unknown; quoted by Adam Black.)

Passed Participles *n.phr.* Game of puntifical poetic justice. (John Fuller calls it "Firing the Fireman": Espy, 1975, "20 August: Word Belt." In Spanish; *Bombear el bombero.*) Its premise; jobholders are variously discharged, to make the punishment fit the crime. One could say that bankers risk being discredited, cowboys deranged, electricians delighted, grass dealers disjointed, homebrew artists distilled, linebackers deballed, longhaired models distressed, mathematicians disfigured, printers depressed, teachers detested, tailors depleated, furriers disabled, dictators overruled, superstars defamed, equestrians derided.

But the term covers other disasters too: activists being deliberated, brides dismissed, drunks disbarred, jocks unstrapped, nudists recovered, revivalists and mediums dispirited.

Thereafter, martial law requires a devoted electorate: and until Hercules rescued him, Prometheus was daily delivered.

Brandreth lists 45 similar examples, with possibly some duplication (*More Joy of Lex:* Wm. Morrow 1982)

Cynic *n.* 1) These days, a realist. 2) An idealist whose rose colored glasses have been knocked off once too often. 3) Any child lied to, cheated, betrayed, or abused often enough by trusted adults. 4) One who refuses to pretend to see the Emperor's new clothes. (*Eccl.* 4:13.) 5) One who agrees with other definitions found herein. Some are born cynical, some achieve cynicism, others have cynicism thrust upon them.

"We the unwilling, led by the unknowing, are doing the impossible for the ungrateful," — (T-shirt slogan, NYC, 1975.)

Cynic's Dictionary *n.phr.* 1) Truth with a grin and sometimes a grimace. 2) An analysis of the obvious with some results that aren't; or results that aren't obvious to some. 3) Contradictionary of dogma. Intended to start people thinking differently about thinking differently. 4) Righteous indignation distilled for forty years. 5) Good bathroom reading; a cleansing experience. 6) Source of the word play herein.

A quick tip o' the foolscap to Walter Redfern, who wrote the book about *Puns* (Oxford: Basil Blackwell, 1984). Others to those many good people who fed me some of the more outrageous lines; the ubiquitous Pete Moss (whom we all knew in high school), Archie Pelligo and everyone in his group, our friends

HOME GROAN

— A —

accident Offspring of the loaded gun by the loaded hunter; of the loaded car by the loaded driver.

accountant Bookcook. Sometimes they provoke the ire of the IRS.

acne Zit happens. "Damn this acne!" Tom shouted rashly.

actor *Lear* today, gone tomorrow.

addict One who believes that while there's life there's dope. Crave slave

addiction Stark craving mad. Brain Chain

aerobics The joy of pecs.

airport Terminal architecture for the upward mobile.

alarm clock "Eine kleine Achtsmusik."

ACTOR
Lear today, gone tomorrow.

alcohol At the steering wheel, sobriety is the price of life. Was this sip necessary?

alcoholic Tight nut behind a steering wheel. His amorous affairs are often close encounters of the slurred kind: "Better to have lushed and lost than never to have lushed at all." A mind is a terrible thing to baste.

alcoholism Gradual liquidation of the mind. Where no booze is good news.

America For bible-thumpers, the land of the spree and the home of the knave. Under Christian Right theocracy, it would become the land of debris and the home of the slave.

American Way Of Life The Law and the Profits. Initials A.W.O.L. = "Avarice WithOut Limit."

analogy "Ah, but a man's speech must exceed his grasp, or what's a metaphor?"

anorexia A waist is a terrible thing to mind.

antibiotics What you give the one who has everything.

antichrist "Christians dislike the Great Beast of Revelations because he's oversixed."

ALCOHOLIC
"Better to have lushed and lost
than never to have lushed at all."

aquarium House of gill repute.

archaeology Rubble rousing. "Archaeologists date any old thing." — (Bumpersticker, 1985)

architecture Sometimes, the Wright stuff.

Arizona "Land of the flea, home of the plague." —(Bumpersticker, circa 1986). Aridzona as the Greeks pronounce it. To them that word would mean "superbelt," perhaps a chastity belt.

Armageddon Going out in a craze of glory.

arms dealers Merchants of Vengeance.

arson Flame Game.

artificial insemination Population without copulation.

ascribed status/genealogy Man does not live by bred alone.

ashtray Crock full o'butts.

asylum Block full o'nuts.

atheism A religion whose chief dogma is "There is no God and Madalyn Murray O'Hair is his prophet." Soviet Marxism's version: "Let icons be bygones."

atomic bomb Dangerous fissions.

AUM Brahma is AUMnipotent.

aviary House of trill repute.

— B —

baboon Arse of another color.

backpacking The joy of treks.

bagels Chewish pastry. Often found under the sign of torus.

baldness Fallout problem.

ballooning Expensive legal high. Uplifting experience. "Down with gravity." — Balloonists' toast.

bankers The Loan Arranger. Too often their vaults outweigh their virtues. "You say I'm overdrawn?" asked Tom incredulously.

bankruptcy Fate worse than debt.

barbarian A dark and stormy knight. His moral law is a code of deathics. From gruesome to *Groo*some; by turn Conan, Gonad and Conehead. (If it's Conan, give me Doyle.) "Beserkers do it without thinking." —(Button, circa 1984.)

barbershop Legal clip joint.

BABOON
Arse of another color.

bargain Where GOOD BUYS should be spelled GOODBYE$.

bargain hunting Going off the cheap end.

barnyard Fowl-smelling area. Where young chicks become old hens. Where roosters boast, "Cock-enough-for-two!" and hens reply, "Talktalk-talktalk . . ."

baseball Going batty. Where stealing bases is not a crime but a crowd pleaser. Where popping flies is not a private pastime but a public practice. At worst, the throws of agony.

basketball The only place where dribble isn't something to wipe off. Old basketballers never die; they just dribble away.

bastard A growing population. A bungle of joy.

baths The public kind has been called Gland Central Station.

battles Formerly the music of the spears.

beard For conservatives, a chin of iniquity.

Beatles Some of the best cheers of our lives.

BALDNESS
Fallout problem.

beauty contests Where Leer is King. Contestants are often bustboasters.

bee Nectar collector. Killer bees are the answer to, "Death where is thy sting?"

beer Mug's game. At first, the cup that cheers; later, the stein of least resistance; then, the cup that blears. Beer today, gone tomorrow. More often a fly-opener than an eye-opener.

behavior modification Shock around the clock.

belts Clothes encounters of the gird kind.

bestiality Peterasty. Getting it on with the Playmutt of the Month. Source of sheep thrills. "It's me and ewe, baby!"

bible Guilt-edged anthology. The greatest story ever sold.

big wheel Forever running around in circles making an axle of himself.

Bikini No man's land.

bill Dread letter.

bird Nutcracker tweet. Source of cheep trills.

BARNYARD
Fowl-smelling area.
Where young chicks become old hens.

birdseed The joy of pecks.

birth control Copulation without population. Use on every conceivable occasion. "Use Contraceptives: No Deposit, No Return." (Bumpersticker, circa 1967)

bisexuals In San Francisco, Castro convertibles. Everywhere, those for whom a miss is as good as a male. Always, those unafraid to take a walk on the Wilde side.

bitch Wuff wife. Better with a cold nose than a cold heart. Life's a bitch when you marry one.

black hole Incredible Shrinking Span.

blue laws Those which make Sunday a day of arrest

body language The hardest kind to lie in.

book The write stuff. Take me to your reader (common library sign).

bordello Menage a twat. Another kind of shooting gallery.

bore One who goes on and on while his hearers go yawn and yawn.

BEER
Mug's game. Beer today, gone tomorrow.

Boston What Hath Cod Wrought?

Boutique Frilling station.

boxing Sock exchange. Beating the meat. Consciousness razing.

bread At best, flour power. Often, loaf at first sight. Man does not live by spread alone.

breasts Often, tit to be Fied. "Stay posted for further developments." — (T-shirt on 13-year-old, circa 1969)

bribe The wrong arm of the law. Pearls to pigs.

bridge A span for all seasons.

budget Living below your yearnings. What you stay within by going without.

bug What did one bug say to the other bug? "Let's commit insex." (Source? ... Did I hear that, Wright?)

buggery For sexists, the right peg in the wrong hole. Different pokes for different folks.

bulimia Where the pain in gain lays mainly in the drain.

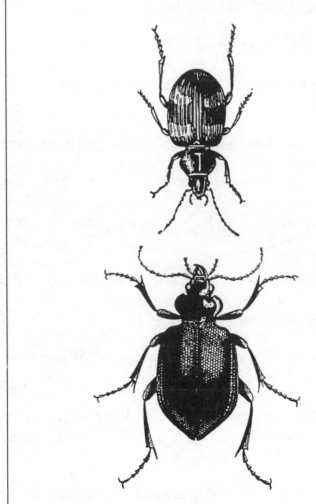

BUG
Q. What did one bug say to the other bug?
A. "Let's commit insex."

bull Cows' spouse. Beast that plays a bigger role in politics than the donkey or elephant. Steer today, gone tomorrow. "Don't be cowed: it's only a lot of bull." — (Button, circa 1988)

bustle Rear-view falsies.

— C —

calendar A tyrant one cannot depose; nevertheless, its days are numbered.

campaign promises Like piñatas and eggshells, made to be broken. Most should be labeled with the usual dangerous drug warnings: "For external use only, Avoid contact with eyes, If swallowed induce vomiting."

cannibalism Mankind's closet skeletons. "Am I my brother's kipper?" — (Robert Bloch)

canopic jar Crock full o' guts.

capitalism Moneytheism. (Jay Cantor called it "Keepitallism.") Fertility cult for money. Its guru is the Prophet Motive whose mantra is, "Buy Low, Sell High."

capital punishment Its defenders believe that none but depraved deserve the chair.

car A vroom with a view. Seat of driving passions. Crashes to ashes and rust to dust. Help Keep the

W in Wreckless Driving. "Faster than a speeding ticket." — (Bumpersticker, 4/90, CA)

cartoon Epigram in line — sometimes out of line. Why the pen IS sometimes mightier than the sword.

casino House of shill repute.

casting couch Occupants need not ask for whom the swell roles.

castration Farmers' ball game. At worst, dehorning. Moral Turkitude. The gonads on the grass, alas.

cats Mewsic makers. Furry purries and prowly yowlys. The best grant close encounters of the purred kind; the worst are short for catastrophies. Appealing to purrient interests. What a difference a spay makes. (Schrodinger's cat may have been a Missing Lynx, but eventually a dead certainty.)

CBW Acronym for Cruelty Beyond Warrant. Each supplier of materiel is a Merchant of Venoms.

cemetery Morgue-aged property. O grave new world that has such people in it.

censor The Grim Bleeper. The Banishing American. His motto: "To swear is human, to bleep, divine." "Sinners?" asked the Censor. / "Sinners!" cried the Censor. "Contention, apprehension and detention must begin!"

censorship Burning issue. Genocide of ideas: "better dead than read." By turns gang-ban and gag-bang. X-clusion act. A ban for all seasons. The Great Brain Robbery.
  "Would you say that Orville & Wilbur were a pair of Wright wingers?" / "No, just plane people." "DeLaurentiis and Fellini are reel people." / "Then movie censors are unreel people." / "No, they're too real." / "Yes, and their motto is 'To reel or not to reel'." — (NYU graffiti, 1979)

champagne Wine of least resistance. Champagne tonight, real pain tomorrow. "Champagne to my real friends and real pain to my sham friends." —(Toast, quoted by Pete Moss)

charity Man does not give by bread alone.

chaste Past tense of an unsuccessful chase. Hence, Chased in vain. "Chaste makes waist." — (Isaac Bonewits)

chess The joy of checks.

chicken Inmate of a cockcentration camp or a henitentiary. To Chinese, the lowliest rooster can become the cock of the wok, no longer singing a cheep arrangement of "Why is everybody pecking on me?" If a gossip's cackle is an ego trip, a chicken's is an eggotrip.

chickenshit Cacadoodledoodoo.

child At best a giggly wriggly. At worst, the harmless necessary brat.

childcare A crying need.

chocolate "Chocolate decadence," said Tom sweetly.

Christian Right Often, hardsell Baptists.

Christmas shopping Yulebesorry

Christmas spirit Too often, Alchollydaze.

Church *Chacun à son pew.*

CIA The Great Unwatched. You can't judge a spook by its cover.

cigar Money to burn. To capitalists, the sweet smell of success. How a man becomes a were-dragon, the Grim Reeker.

CHICKEN
Death row prisoner
in a cockcentration camp or a henitentiary.

cigarettes If you must smoke, don't breathe it to a soul. Coffin nails. "Listen to that chronic smoker coffin."

cirrhosis Hearse of the drinking class. Hearse of a different choler

class struggle Us vs. Us masquerading as Us vs. Them. How can We survive that? "I work so my boss doesn't have to." — (Button, 1989)

cleanliness Often, next to oddliness. Why the USA has become a nation of soap addicts. "Some day my rinse will come." "Dull people have immaculate homes." — (welcome mat slogan).

clean mind A result of brainwashing. "Clean mind, clean body . . . Take your pick." (button slogan)

clergy Too often, cope addicts. Jesus and his disciples were carpenters, fishermen, etc., each with his altar ego. Too often, cope, chasuble & cassock are the Drapes of Wrath.

cliché Old saw with blunted teeth. Not only verbal chewing gum but also an anagram of chicle. Nerd words.

clinic House of pill repute.

CIGAR
Money to burn. The Grim Reeker.

clock Another tyrant one cannot depose. But fear not, its hours are numbered. Though usually no more reliable than its maker, it settles arguments without saying a word. Unlike its victims, it runs for hours without needing its face and hands washed. Life's yardtick.

clothes Meat wrappers. Different cloaks for different folks. They cover a multitude of skins. To wear is human. Man does not live by thread alone. "As ye sew so shall ye rip."

clown The Grin Reaper.

cocaine For too many, the line of least resistance. Addict's motto: The toot, the whole toot, and nothing but the toot. "My other car is up my nose." (License plate frame, CA, 1989.)

cocktail party Where allegedly tight makes right and vice versa. In dress and drink alike, the name of the game is blend.

cockteaser Roger dodger.

codpiece Peter Pad. Hard sell advertisment.

coffee For many, the cup that clears. "Caffiend." —(Button, 1988) "This coffee is awful," said Tom bitterly.

collection agency House of bill repute. Dread letter office. Appropriate motto: This Dun For Hire.

Colorado Beauty is in the skys over Boulder.

commercials Dangerous fictions. Close encounters of the absurd kind.

committee Where minutes are taken and then read while hours are lost.

competition Stress for success.

computer Often, a Mac of all trades. Hackers Köen: "Are you programming the machine or is the machine programming you?"
   "Lisp is a recursive language. First you curse, Then you recurse." — (Button, circa 1988)
   "Floppy now, hard later" — (Graffito, Silicon Valley)

condoms Tubesteak wrappers. Losing your erection when it's time to put on the condom makes it the French letter than killeth.
   Q: Why are condoms like the Republican Party? /A: Because they stand for inflation; they halt production, and they give you a false sense of security while you're getting screwed.

confiscated Rendered unto Seizer. Subjected to a hostile takeover.

conformity Fashion Passion.

conspiracy Collusions of grandeur.

contract The bind that ties.

conversion Sects change operation.

cooperation The pacts of life.

coronation The reigny day a monarchy saves for.

corporal punishment The whacks of life. Devotees think a switch in time saves nine and too many think more is better. This punishment for you. What the sergeant gave his underling.

corset Its wearer is a build in a girdled cage. Again, a waist is a terrible thing to mind.

cosmetics Bleaches and cream. Paint for lilies. Meant to make young girls look older sooner and their mothers look younger longer. Therefore, ask not for whom the belle kohls. She kohls for thee.

costume Clothes by any other name, of any other place or time. Sowing wild coats. Puttin' on the glitz. Sometimes wings and things and buttons and bows.

cottage cheese Having a whey with curds. *Chacun à son goop.*

country lane The road less gravelled.

court Where *lawyers* becomes a mispronounciation of *liars;* where justice may be blind and deaf; where sentences are a matter of trial and terror.

courtship Pulling the woo over her eyes.

cowboy The Grim Roper to the cow.

crack coke smoke. Creator of cracked minds and sometimes cracked heads. The addict is between a rock and a hard place.

crackpot Often more prophet-minded that most businessmen.

creative accounting Ledgerdemain. Doublebook entrykeeping. Book cooking. Fiction that's stranger than truth.

crèche Bornyard.

criminal Fit to be tried. "I did it," Tom confessed guiltily.

criticism A pan for all seasons.

critics Often, jeerleaders. Sometimes, boastbusters. Nothing censured, nothing gained. Taste testers.

cubesteak Result of beating the meat.

cult Faith worse than death.

curiosity Wonderlust.

DANCE
Another kind of playing footsie.

— D —

damn Curse of another choler.

dance Another kind of playing footsie. From mingle jangles to spin of iniquity.

dating Competitive sport, played by the male with phallus aforethought (perceived by some females as phallus intentions).

death Different croaks for different folks.

debauch Originally, exertion desertion; now, libertines' libcrties.

debriefing Letting it all hang out.

declaration of war The letter that killeth.

deism Theology with dilutions of grandeur.

delirium tremens Alcohell.

demolition derby The joy of wrecks. Smashing success.

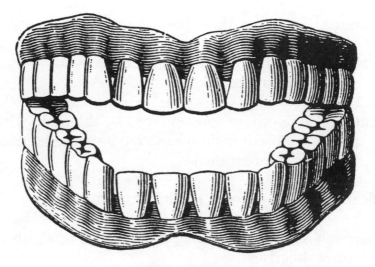

DENTURES
Little white lies.

dentures Little white lies.

deregulation Why airline schedules have become flights of fancy.

dialectic "Where there's a will there's a won't." —(Ambrose Bierce.) "More power to the right wing!" (A Patriot) Which results in a left turn. (A Pilot) —graffiti. As it was in the beginning, is now and ever shall be, whirled without end, Amen.

diet A losing battle. Girth control. Mirth control. Game where losing is winning: "no gain, no pain."

dirty mind Better than none. One for which naked = X-posed.

discord Ideally resolves to dat chord.

Disraeli The greatest Tory ever sold.

dissent Public display of a faction. "Dissent the right thing to do."

divorce The joy of ex. The mutiny before the bounty. Split happens.

divorcee Ex-rated.

dog The pup that cheers. If you treat a man like a dog, don't be surprised if he acts like a S.O.B.

doggerel Often preserved by caterwauling.

dogma Often imparted by catechism. Let sleeping dogmas lie (and vice versa).

Don Juan A grope addict. A dally slave. A lasshopper. A Big Dame Hunter who will settle for any.

doughnuts Rolling Scones. Often found under the sign of torus.

Dracula A neck romancer.

drag Male fraud. Improper form of a dress.

dress On a manikin, a short shift; elsewhere, Statutory drape. The sacks of wife.

drive-in movie Wall-to-wall car petting.

drug testing Urine trouble. Jar Wars. Search for the incontinent.

drunk Brain drained.

drunk driving From beer to eternity.

drunkspeak Schlitz of the tongue. After too many Wild Turkeys sounding like a domestic one.

ducks The quacks of life.

duel Traditionally, the Grim Rapier or two-party Russian roulette. Another way to get a bang out of life.

Dungeons & Dragons® A game where dice play gods with the universe. "Life's a die and then you bitch." — (Button/T-shirt, 1988)

duty Is in the eye of the upholder.

— E —

earth The mother we abuse everyday. The home we treat like dirt.

earthquakes Great quakes from little forewarns grow.

ecocide The Fall of the Wild. Devaluation of Planet Worth. Creating the nozone layer. "Go waste, young man."

ecumenical Learning to get along with the opposite sects.

efficiency expert Sloth sleuth.

Egypt Dat Sadat!

election A Pollish joke. Calling an election a "landslide" is calling voters a lot of clods. Alienation of a faction. Popularity contest in Camp Aignland. "The trouble with political jokes is that they get elected." (graffito NYC, circa 1984)

Empire State Building Al Smith's last erection.

encyclicals Disseminated papal bull.

enema Tush flush for a purge urge.

enemy Foes by any other name.

entertainment Covers a multitude of sings.

epigram Notable quotable. Flip quip.

epitaphs "All too often grave errors," said Tom cryptically

erection Flash in the pants. Pocket rocket. The original Tower of Power. The stiff of life, the staff of laugh, and often vice versa. Sowing machine. Glandstand play. A male body's most honest compliment: Totally tubular. Being too big for one's breeches. Organic lollipop. For sexists, a beaver cleaver, a pocket screwdriver. Sproing fever. "Nine inches!" said Tom cockily. "Will the Real Tricky Dick Please Stand Up?"
    Draft shaft, Prod rod, Wad rod, Condomized: a shod rod. To feminists, the original Boob Tube.

erotica All the screws that fit the print.

erotophobia countercockwise mindset. No quiffs, stands, or butts.

euthanasia Taking your life into your hands. Oriental lad or lass.

exercise At best, the joy of flex.

experiment Bridge over the River Try.

expert A real knowbody.

exploration Prehistoric joy of treks

extinction To a behaviorist, pulling habits out of rats.

exurbs I say it's Greenwich and I say the hell with it.

— F —

fad In one year and out the other.

falsies Delusions of glandeur.

fame Hero today, gone tomorrow.

farmer's daughter Dairy Queen. "She sits among the cabbages and peas."

fart Both natural gas and a backfire. To pass crass ass gas. A bowel growl. By turns, a weak squeak from a whiny heinie or a foul howl from a heinous anus. Sometimes how you spell RELIEF, and why BEAN is a four letter word. At worst, an est-hole assertion. *Chacun à son phew.* "Fart for Fart's sake." — (Graffito, Berkeley, CA 1990)

fashion Comedy of wearers. Fit to be eyed. The original flourish of strumpets. Among businessmen, the bland leading the bland. Among the hip, gear today, gone tomorrow. Do rear ends justify the jeans? Q: What do a cheap hotel and tight jeans have in common? A: No ballroom.

FAT
Adipose complex.
Why a waist is a terrible thing to mind.

fat Adipose complex. Where the pain in Jane flays mainly in the gain. Why a waist is a terrible thing to mind.

fatcat Holder of the purr strings.

fear Man does not live by dread alone.

feghoot "If puns were baloney, this would be the wurst."

fellation Making the piss pipe into the peace pipe. "This Pud's For You." *Chacun à son goo.* "If God hadn't meant for us to suck cock, why did He make it look like a popsicle?" (U.Wisc. graffito.)

fencing Out to lunge. Motto: In God We Thrust. Themesong: I'm just wild about parry. Official organ: *Saturday Evening Riposte.* Fencer's damn: "Curses! Foiled Again!"

fetish Sexual synecdoche: taking the part for the hole.

fibre Bran for all seasons.

fickle Dear today, gone tomorrow.

fight What a difference a fray makes.

FENCING
Out to lunge. Motto: In God We Thrust.

fire One could say that a pyromaniac is arson around. Fax Vobiscum = "May the Torch be with you."

fireworks Money to burn.

fishing Making the best of a bass situation. O tempura, O morays.

flattery Gloze by any other name.

flirt Dame game.

flirting Wishful winking.

flogging The scrapes of wrath. What a difference a flay makes.

florists Petal pushers.

folk music Too often, sung in the key of Off.

foreplay Tickle relish. The other 96% of sex. In the bath, committing sudomy.

fossil Stone of contention. The real rock of ages.

fraternity Too often, the frat pack is more Geek than Greek.

FOLK MUSIC
Too often, sung in the key of Off.

free love Better than any kind you can buy. *Shack-up à son goût.* (Graffito, Berkeley, 1960's)

freeway Colossus of Roads. Q: Why do so many turkeys drive? A: Because they're too stupid to fly.

French kiss Keeping a civil tongue in another's mouth.

friends The best peers of our lives.

fuck Pant counterpant, becoming a glandslide.

fucking Moving and shaking. Doing it the hard way. Desire in pursuit of the hole.

fundamentalism Total mythapprehension. Moral twerpitude.

GAY
Bedroom Outlaw. Forbidden fruit.

— G —

gagwriter Denizen of a quip joint. Sharpener of old saws. Courtless jester. Both feeder of the lines and man behind the routines.

gamble Splurge urge.

gay Bedroom Outlaw. Forbidden fruit. Gays are less often white punks on dope than bright hunks on hope.

geneaology Remembrance of Flings Past. Man does not live by bred alone.

ghost Eerie today, gone tomorrow. Bansheets. Pooka Boo!

gifted children Whys beyond their years.

glossolalia Holy Babble. When enough do it together, Holy Babel.

gluttony Mea gulpa, mea gulpa, mea maxima gulpa.

gobbledygook Turkey talk. Decomposing tongue.

GOLFER
Jock full o' putts.

gold coins Like other eagles, extinct species. Some were creations of Augustus St. Gaudy.

golfer Jock full o' putts.

gossip Let the chat out of the bag. Too often, manifest an interferiority complex. Smear today, gone tomorrow.

gossip columnists Writers of wrongs.

graduation At worst, letting the brat out of the bag.

graffiti Left-on writeon. The handwriting on the wall. "These graffiti are off the wall." (East Village, 1982) DO NOT DROP. — Reputedly painted on a nuke warhead.

G-rated Bland for all seasons.

greed The joy of cheques.

guilt The delusion that the Maker of 100 billion galaxies personally gives a damn what or whom you crave. "God made love. Man made guilt. Whom do YOU trust?" Wishful sinking. Repent, a friend might hear!

gun Man does not live by lead alone. "This house protected by Smith & Wesson" — (Mailbox sticker, MS 1966) Why a drink is preferable to a shot. Either a big bore or a small bore, but hard to ignore. "The family that shoots together, loots together" (Graffito, LA 1992)

— H —

habeas corpus Right of spring.

haberdashery House of twill repute. "Pants half off" —(Store sign, Berkeley, CA 1990)

hacker One of the Mac pack. One for whom a computer can inspire love at first byte.

haircut / hairdo Shear nonsense. Often, fit to be dyed.

hate It is not given to man to loathe and be wise.

Hawaii A great place to get lei'd. Surfus Maximus.

hazing The shove that dare not tell its name.

H-bomb Dangerous fissions.

heartland Home on the grange. National paunch, restrained by the Bible belt.

heaven According to its loudest press agents, to get there you must turn right, keep straight, and expect to go through a lot of hell enroute.

heresy trial cope opera.

hero The operatic Siegfried is Conan the Wagnerian.

history In one era and out the other. Not limited to Remembrance of Kings Past.

hockey Pucking around.

Hollywood The Fief of Badgag.

homeopathy Mind over medicine. Dilutions of grandeur. "Fix me up, Herb."

homework The curse of the thinking class.

hooker Feemale. Peter patter. Male order business partner.

horny Up and coming.

horror movies Cheap chills. Where 'tis the season to be crawley.

hospitals Bedpanorama.

hot pants Breeches of promise.

hot tub Different soaks for different folks.

hung Better to be well hung than well hanged.

hustler Rent-a-cock.

hypocrisy Paying lip service to honesty.

hysterectomy American Spay of Wife.

— I —

ideology "Like most movements, it eventually needs to be flushed."

impotent Having can'ts in the pants.

inaugural ball Foreplay to a four-year screwing.

incest Having the kin you love to touch. Sometimes, by turns, sibling ribaldry, sibling revelry.

income tax Bite of spring. Often more than Shakespearean "3,000 dolours a year." (*Measure for Measure* I ii 50.) Why April 15 is the rainy day we must save for.

incumbent Lying on top: said of undeposed politicians.

infidelity Confusing lay and lie.

inhibited Tied up in nots.

innuendo Allegerdemain.

Inquisition Rack around the clock.

insulted Taken aback by an affront.

intensive care unit Womb with a view.

interior decorators Light and shady characters

Iraq Its last decade's TV coverage has been the Iraqui Horror Picture Show.

Ireland Brogues' gallery

JESTER
Secular humorist. . .
"Don't give up the quip."

— J —

jazz Sax appeal.

jester Secular humorist. He aims Apollo's arrows at the jocular vein. He gives us some of the best jeers of our lives. He offers us truths with a grin assault. His occupational hazard is scherzophrenia. His motto might well be "Don't give up the quip."

jihad Clash of symbols. Where allegedly fight makes right.

job From hire to infirmity.

jockstrap Ballpark

jogging Change of pace and vice versa.

— K —

Karl Marx KM's grave is just another Communist plot. If it's Karl, give me Popper; if it's Marx, give me Groucho.

karma The waves you make, the acts of life. Causes effect; convictions convict; possessions possess.

kennel Curgatory.

kids The best dears of our lives.

king Hankering (like Plato) for a wise one is seeking Solomon to watch over me. Among the fundamentalists' wicked kings, many fear Thin__ worse than Drin__, Smo__, Fuc__.

King Kong An urban gorilla.

kiss Look before you lip.

kittens Cat litter you don't throw out.

Knowledge No brain, no gain. "Learning is a gray matter," said Tom wisely.

Kremlin Tsar Chamber

Ku Klux Klan Out to lynch. Rebel rousers. A religion of Kludd and blunder.

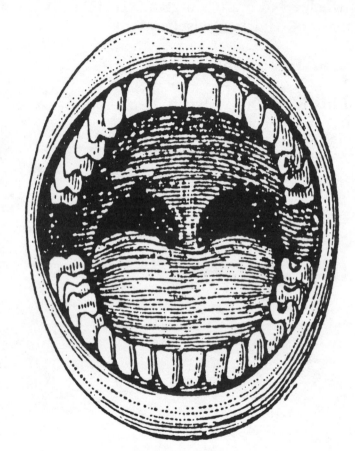

LAUGHTER
Clonic tonic.

— L —

labor of love Childbirth.

LaBrea Wall-to-wall tarpits.

Lamont Cranston The original 5 o'clock Shadow.

landlord Too often the lessor of 2 evils: too high rent, too little maintenance

lap Best seat in the house.

lapdogs Close encounters of the furred kind.

laughter Clonic tonic. Black humor is the Dark Side of the Farce, not the whole show. Laughing matters.

leer Screwtiny. Glance askance. Grin of iniquity.

lie "I only tell the truth" Pinocchio said nosily.

limerence Merge urge. Preoccupational hazard. Sowing wild dotes. When one feels like a yearning urn for spurning hunk.

LOVE
Caring and sharing. Buddy building.

limerick Often, vice verse.

literary agent Often not a gent. Purveyor of wordly goods. By name, Author Gadfly.

liposuction Letting the fat out of the bag.

lobbyists PAC-men.

Los Angeles The Desolation of Smog.

louse Nit happens.

love Caring and sharing. Buddy building.

love duet Making beautiful music together. "Why Don't We Duet in the Road?"

LSD Not automatically a Satori night special. "Don't Give Up The Trip."

lynch law trial by fury.

— M —

Macavity Purrfect alibi.

machismo Stud and blunder.

mad scenes Operatic: choleratura.

mainlining Vein pursuit.

male chauvinist Often, a wash-and-wear wolf.

male supremacy When a vas deferens makes a vast difference.

man Dog's best friend. The same leash holds dog and master: too often a bitch on one end, a S.O.B. on the other.

marijuana The original "flower power." Getting a bhang out of life. Nature's way of saying "High!" Often, playing hookah. Going potty. Shared token of approval.

marital duty Part of the high cost of loving.

market Bourse of another color.

marriage For males, a wife sentence. Altar'd state. Man does not live by wed alone. "Holy Matrimony, Batman! You mean I have to hurry up and find a wife?" In a A GRIM REAPER.

martini Gin of iniquity.

martyrdom Bleedership.

masochism Infinite capacity for taking pains — in context. Giving it up = going off the beaten path.

massage The joy of necks. Meeting need by kneading meat.

masturbation Organ solo learned by even the musically untalented. Sometimes, the sound of one hand clapping.

mathematics The best numbers game. Where fractions speak louder than surds.

midnight When both hands are up.

mimic It takes one to show one.

missionary position American Lay of Wife.

monastery Consecration camp.

MARTINI
Gin of iniquity.

Moral Majority Pride goeth before a Falwell.

motorcycle How they do it in the dirt. Something hot between your legs. Different spokes for different folks. Too often, the ride that goeth before a fall.

Mt.St.Helens Mother Nature getting her rocks off and making an ash of herself.

movies Splice of life.

music Often earidescence. At worst, the caterwauling that preserves doggerel.

myopia Hocus focus.

mysteries At the climax of a whodunit, it's Howdy Doodit Time.

NECKTIE
Different chokes for different folks.

— N —

napalm Rain of terror.

national anthems Jingo jingles.

necktie Different chokes for different folks.

nest Home tweet home. Nutcrackers' suite.

neurotic Tied up in nots.

noise Earitation.

Norway Live by the fjord die by the fjord

novels Too often, plotboilers.

nuclear exchange Again, dangerous fissions. I'll show
you mine if you show me yours. My pop is bigger
than yours. No nukes is good nukes. "Come on,
Baby, light my pyre."

nuclear war Boom & doom. Where all men are
cremated equal. "Don't blow it. Good planets are
hard to find."

nuclear winter Hell freezing over. Possibly preventable by a nuclear freeze.

nude Wearing a one-button suit. Nude skydiving: the height of exhibitionism.

nudist camp Comedy of barers. "Don't give up the strip."

— O —

obsession Preoccupational hazard. PB at best, habitual ritual.

onion Garden variety tearjerker.

opera At worst, Lucia di Yammermore. Sometimes, Remembrance of Rings Past. *Lohengrin:* peer today, gone tomorrow. The urge to burst into song after it's over is the Placido Effect.

opposition The breakfast of champions.

optimist A hope addict.

oral sex The original Naked Lunch. "I never liked flies till I opened one." — (T-shirt, 1984.) So Do Me. —(1967 button slogan)

orgasm Gland finale. Where push comes to shove. Tumescence quintessence. Erection ejection. Sometimes, how you spell Relief. "Love comes in spurts." "To go together is blessed. To come together is divine."

OPERA
Lucia di Yammermore.

orgy Swap meat. Class snuggle. Fourplay. "Asses to asses and bust to bust / If th' rod won't salve you, the revel must." "One man's meat is another's person." "What if they gave an orgy and nobody came?"

out-takes Image trimage. Often, film flam. The Last of the Deletions.

Oxymoron: Holy Roman Empire. Practical Joke. Marital Bliss. Children's rights. Criminal Justice. Prisoners' Rights.

— P —

pants For males, statutory drape. "Pants Half Off!" —(Berkley, store slogan).

pantyhose Sheer today gone tomorrow.

Paris Partly in Seine.

parka Foul-weather friend.

past participle Game of puntifical poetic justice, a.k.a. Firing the Fireman. Bankers risk being discredited, cowboys deranged, electricians delighted, grass dealers disjointed, homebrew artists distilled, linebackers deballed, longhaired models distressed, mathematicians disfigured, printers depressed, teachers detested, and bribetaking police disgruntled.

Activists risk being deliberated, brides dismissed, drunks disbarred, jocks unstrapped, mediums and revivalists dispirited. Thereafter, martial law requires a devoted electorate; and until Hercules rescued him, Prometheus was daily delivered.

pejoratives Slur words: fleers, jeers and sneers.

penis Mightier than the sword. Organic lawn sprinkler.

perfumes Skincense.

perjury Sowing wild oaths.

pheromones Escentials.

pickle works House of dill repute. "What did they soak thee in?" cried Tom sourly

pig The sty's the limit.

pimp Bawdyguard. Nookie bookie: guilty of miss management.

piss Make the bladder gladder. How you spell Relief. "When nature calls, people listen."

plague Epidamnic. Pox vobiscum. "A plague on both your houses."

plastic surgery When beauty is nip and tuck. "You look as good as new," said Tom falsely.

play Take a walk on the child side.

PIG
The sty's the limit.

pollution "It's my least favorite of the Great Lakes," said Tom eerily.

playground Kid row.

poetry Words that sing and dance, swing and prance: nearer to chant than chance, to prayer than to prose. At worst, from bad to verse: from Orpheus to Morpheus.

politicians The most powerful ones are blockheads. Liars and Tyrants and Snares, Oh My!

population pressure Force of habitat.

pornographer Proprietor of a grossery.

pornography Gross national product. In the I of the beholder. Friction fiction. Spurts pages. Coming attractions. Adult bedtime stories.
    Q: Why is porn like churches? A: Because no one type satisfies everyone and even the weirdest types satisfy some.

poverty Outwageous condition. Acquired Income Deficiency Syndrome.

power Might makes fright.

practical joke Neither. Wit to be Fie!'d.

POLITICIANS
The most powerful ones are bloc heads.

preemptive offensive First strike, worst strike.

pregnancy The shape of things to come. Bonus dividend for regular deposits. Womb service. From here to maternity. Having fecund thoughts. The Fax of life.

premature ejaculation Going off half-cocked.

prick The Grim Raper.

prison House of kill repute.

Prophecy "Yes, I wrote the *Lamentations*," said Jeremiah woefully.

profit Greed feed.

proofreaders Galley slaves.

propaganda Misrepresentational art. Better dead than read.

prostitution Pay as you come. Sex in the mercenary position. Cashual sex. At best, a pig in a poke; at worst, vice versa.

prudery Penile dementia. Having shan'ts in the pants.

psychosurgery A hole in the head. "Better a free bottle in front o'me than a prefrontal lobotomy."

puberty A hair-raising experience. First gush, first crush, first rush.

public opinion By turns a sacred cow and a lot of bull.

pun Is mightier than the word. Word jazz, by which a jingle of phonemes becomes a jangle of themes; a jungle of seemings, a juggle of meanings: chance transfigured by choice, where virtue is its own reword. Linguistic fusion energy. Epigram epitomized; comedy condensed; even an odd maxim minimized. Its beauty is in the Oy! of the beholder.

punster Cunning linguist whose tongue plays games provoking moans and groans. Our prey is the clichémonger: "In your heart you know he's trite." The punster's preferred demise? Digesting.

pushmepullyou Palindromedary.

pussy A little mound of fur one wants to pet.

— Q —

quarrel The joy of vex. The parties consist of at least one with fingers in ears and at least one with foot in mouth; they often exchange roles. Soothe is stronger than friction. Spurred words.

quickie Bang, bang, you're bred.

QUARREL
The joy of vex. . .
Soothe is stronger than friction.

— R —

racism A force of a different color. Origin sin. Looking at black and white and seeing red.

racist One who acts as if he thought Jesus meant "By their Roots ye shall know them."

rape Insertion coercion.

rapture "You mean we spend the next seven years in the clouds?" asked Tom rapturously.

razor The scrapes of bath. Advocates apparently believe "None but the shaved deserve the fair."

Reagan The man who gave a new meaning to the term "acting president."

rebuttal Goat's revenge.

reality A working hypothesis (Sean Williams). What doesn't vanish when you stop believing in it (Philip K. Dick).

recombinant DNA Designer genes.

red-blooded Describing lustboasters.

red-light district Block full o'sluts.

refrigerator Chilling station.

religions At worst, politics with a halo: *folie a dieux.*

Republican Party Where might makes tight.

restaurant House of fill repute. The non-veggie kind is often a house of grill repute.

restroom Where you rest only at peril of arrest.

retirement The long unwinding mode or worse, the long unwinding mold. Time to kick back and pay tax. Pasturized employees.

revival The joy of sects.

revolution Revolting development: exchange of one tyranny for another.

rock & roll The music that woke the Dead. Often, out to raunch.

romantic Given to idyll worship.

roulette To gamblers, the music of the spheres.

Russian roulette Getting a bang out of life.

RUSSIAN ROULETTE
Getting a bang out of life.

— S —

sacred cow Baloney in drag.

sadist Whip or slapper. One who always demeans what he flays.

sailor Wave slave

SCA (Society for Creative Anachronism) Neo-medieval theatre of the absurd. Where a duke outranks a king. Its costumery: sewing wild coats for poor beknighted folk and their ladies. Young squires' motto: "There's a sword in your future."

scatology Turd words. Shit Wit.

science Ideally, humanity's collective bullshit filter. In practice, the truth, but neither the whole truth nor nothing but the truth.

science fiction Fiction of the future and vice versa. Stories of the where & when, free of the limits of the here & now or of the there & then, which dare to give to what never existed a name and address. Playing God for fun & profit: creating worlds others can safely visit. Paradox regained, regaled, and retailed.

scolding Baptism of ire. The chide that goeth before a brawl.

scriptorium House of quill repute.

self-made man Devout worshipper of his creator. Devotee of his religion's profits.

semen The original controlled substance. The White Stuff. Good to the last drop. Said to be more blessed to give than to receive. The original Ecstaseeds. "The French navy hasn't been feared since the days of Napoleon's semen."

sequins The joy of flecks.

serendipity Bargainhunter's reward. Beachcomber's daily bread. Optimist's justification, pessimist's windfall: booty is in the eye of the beholder.

sex Where overwork leads to underachievement. Getting off by getting it on; not limited to getting it in and out. "Love thy neighbor but don't get caught."

sexism "I'm God's gift to women," said Tom cockily

sextet The joy of six. Making beautiful music together.

sexual orientation Likestyle. A matter of taste and smell. Different pokes for different folks.

sheep Close encounters of the herd kind. Sheared today, gone tomorrow. "It's me & ewe, baby" (Pat MacGregor). Give Fleece a Chance.

shit Apes' weapon where a turd in the hand is worth two in the bush.

shitwork Chores of another color.

shoes Great aches from little toe corns grow.

shop class Where to learn the right tools for getting one's nuts off.

shopping Life's an itch and then you buy. "When you've seen one indoor shopping facility, you've seen the mall" (USENET).

shrinkage Mental result of brainwashing.

silver coins Endangered specie.

SHEEP
Sheared today, gone tomorrow.

sin Heathen pleasure. Whatever you feel guilt about doing. Any behavior fundamentalists dislike. The difference between sin and crime is in which bureaucracy takes offense first.

singles bar Meet rack.

ski Take a powder. Go off the steep end. Often, the slide that goeth before a sprawl. Act as if your motto weren't "Don't Give Up the Flip."

skier Slope addict. Fall guy.

skin Bare essentials.

sleep A doze by any other name. A reward you're unaware of having till it's over.

small talk Civil drivel

smog Lost Horizons. Industrial revelation too often ignored. Long term sighed effect of short term profits.

sneeze Much achoo about nothing.

snowflake Cocaine freak; often a crackpot.

solar energy The original one & only free lunch.

sovereignty The joy of Rex.

spanking Hurting the part that never hurt you. "Ouch!" cried Tom bashfully.

speed A killer, in snorts, pills, injections, or freeways. "There's meth in my madness. / And vice versa." "Give me librium or give me meth." (Graffiti. Last on Cooper Sq., NYC, 1960s.)

stink Disscent.

stockmarket Debenture adventure; by turns a lot of bull in a bear pit and vice versa. Sheep in sheep's clothing.

straight line The shortest distance between two puns.

striptease Damsel in disdress, earning a bare living.

stud Ornamental protuberance. Woodenhead in search of a maidenhead.

subway Wormholes in the Big Apple.

suffering Woes by any other name.

Superman One who can live up to his hype.

sycophant Toady to the max.

synonyms Words of a feather or Nym's transgressions

TENOR
Often, a fubsy mensch.
The best ones are trained to make
their voices at least as big as their egos.

— T —

tail Synecdoche for ass: the part for the hole and vice versa. Sexists usually take it piece by piece.

tan Life's a beach and then you fry.

tangent Digression expression. Departing from a boring subject that tends to run around in circles.

tartan Scotch swatch.

tavern Pour house. Loading zone. Where sooner or later the customer is always tight. Where beer jokes are apt to become brouhahas. Swilling station.

taxation Worth control. Rendering unto Caesar what he thinks should be Caesar's. Life's a leech and then you die. Unlike the taxman, the butcher plucks the chicken only after it is dead. "Aren't you glad you don't get all the government you pay for?" — (Will Rogers.)

tears The original water power.

TOMCAT
More pounce to the ounce.

Technicolor Pigment of the imagination. Reality through the eyes of a child or a tripper.

tenor Often, a fubsy mensch. The best ones are trained to make their voices at least as big as their egos.

Tetragrammaton Greek for a four-letter word. Name of a name of Jehovah. "I'm Tetragrammaton: I am what I am and that's all that I am, I'm Tetragrammaton."

theatre House of thrill repute.

tithing 10% off the top, with a halo: commission paid to Jehovah's self-appointed agents.

tobacco Killer weed.

toga The Sack of Rome.

toilet Unloading zone. Spilling station. Where all the pricks hang out. The Pause that Refreshes.

tomcat More pounce to the ounce. His prayers variously begin "Let us prey" and "Let us spray."

transference Freudianity's born-again experience.

Transvestism Male Fraud

TURKEYS
Nerds of a feather.

trip Biocomputer-enhanced perceptions. Vacation in the psychotropics.

truth Q: What do truth, justice and The American Way of Life have in common? / A: The letter T.

tubesteak Hottest part of the beefcake. "I Want to Hold Your Gland."

turkeys Nerds of a feather.

TV commercials Cravin' images. Buysexual seduction techniques.

tyrant Feared today, gone tomorrow.

— U —

UFOs Flying sorcery. Generic airline foods.

ugly duckling It takes swan to know one.

upper crust A lot of crumbs sticking together.

upward mobility Reckless striving.

— V —

vagina The box a penis comes in.

vampire Noted for a tricky hickey. Hemoglobin junkie. His motto, "Take me to your bleeder."

vanilla sex Taking a walk on the mild side.

vegetarian One who'd rather eat only what couldn't escape. One for whom meat is a 4-letter word.

venereal disease Having a whorible time. Part of the high cost of loving. "Repent ye swingers," said Tom infectuously.

vibrator Politically correct penis. Warmer than a cucumber. To MCPs, the wrong peg in the right hole.

vice squad The Grim Peeper.

viking Norse of another color.

virginity An unprovable negative. Frozen assets. "Virginity is like a balloon: All it needs is one prick and it's gone."

vixen Foxy female or vice versa.

volcanoes Planetary zits. Terminal acne. Why mountains should be seen and not heard. The worst have the highest degrees, Magma Come Loudly.

vote Act done in private among consenting adults. Choice of the lesser evil.

voyeurism "Why is a goose a tickle but a gander only a look?"

— W —

Wall Street Where successful brokers make windfall prophets.

war The Grim Ripper. Shell game, at life and death stakes. Glory with the L knocked out of it. Traditional procedure for deciding not who's right but who's left. In Kuwait, As The World Burns.

warrior The Grim Raper. Bound for gory. Hero today, gone tomorrow.

Washington DC A monstrous spiderweb of lies
Where the spiders and the flies
All wear the same disguise.

W.C. Fields The sot heard round the world.

wedding End of a comedy; often, beginning of a soap opera; too often, of a tragedy. Taking a walk on the aisled side.

weed Unloved plant. Green power. The greening of America. Different tokes for different folks. Devotees are grasshopers and sometimes grassshoppers. They are said to leave no turn unstoned.

W. C. FIELDS
The sot heard round the world.

wet dream Coming unscrewed.

wholesome Bland for all seasons. Euphemism for G-rated.

wine Grape expectations.

winter Froze by any other name. MULTI FRIGENT PAUCI RIGENT "Many are cold but few are frozen."

wizard Grown up whiz kid.

wolf German Sheperd's kissing cousin.

woman What male chauvinists pay lip service to. "A woman without a man is like a river without a dam." Damned if she does, damned if she doesn't, and sometimes vice versa.

WINE
Grape expectations.

—X Y Z—

X-rated Sinema

yes-man One who stoops to concur.

Yule Hollydays. Alcoholidays. Season of "shop till you drop."